A Piece of Mind

Anthony Fox

Presentation by *BookLeaf Publishing*

Web: www.bookleafpub.com

E-mail: info@bookleafpub.com

ISBN: 9789358315424

First edition 2023

In loving memory

Haley Elizabeth Lang

The Little Things

When you were here,
I could have swore that life was perfect.
Now that you are gone,
I cant help but think about
How much better it'd be.
If i had just spent a little more time with you,
Next to me.

From playing with your hair,
or rubbing your feet.
All of those little things
Now mean
so
much,
to
me.

Bearing My Cross

I've got the weight of the world on my shoulders.

I've got to let it go.

I've got to carry my own.

Finding Magick

In the words, there is magic.

In the sounds, there is understanding.

In the actions there is love.

I imagine a new world.
A world where these come together,
to harmonize magnificently.

Faith

When i stray far from home,

i'm never alone.

When i'm up high i might just be

low.

These things i feel the strongest, but

sometimes i feel as if i've never known.

Demons

I've been
wondering
wandering
pondering.

On the possibility
of becoming
an anomaly.

Lost nights and forgotten days.
Grey skies and blue black faces.

I'm trying to hear what they're saying.

Hey kid,
be Patient.
Evil is what you make it,
face it.

Blueberry Bubba spaceship,
take me, away from
all of this fake shit.

Up at night pacing,
heart racing.
I hate it.

Grace

I can feel it now.
The sparks in-between my finger tips.
The high and low tides of the waves that
constitute all things.
There is magic everywhere I look!
Lightning striking from the heavens down into
the balls of my feet.
I am the morning star!
Everything once dark is now light.
I can see it now.
I am you and you are me.
If I bring the light to you,
Oh!, The light shines upon me.

Secrets

They say ignorance is bliss.
However, the veil has been lifted.

Things i've never pondered before, unmasking
themselves in front of me.

I've known forever what they call you.
Yet i have no idea what, or who you are?

Forgive me, but i just want to hold all the
knowledge i've found.
Lock it away, for no one else to see.

These secrets that i keep, one day down the road.
Might just be the key.

Wanderer

When i go far from home i'm never alone,
when i'm up high i might just be low.
These things i feel the strongest but sometimes i
feel as if i've never known.

Alignment

9

I sit.
I be still.
I breathe.
Let the art flow from my heaven down to me.

Reaping

Life is just a dance,
you swing high,
i swing low.

but meet me in the middle and we can just let it
go.

Living

Sinning
Head spinning
Not much grinning.
Just trying to focus on winning.

Voices

I'm like a whisper in the night.
A sudden fright, but oh such a delight.
Burning in fires of joy with much employ.

Dim

When the night is dim and it seems there is no
way to go.
Don't fret, don't even smile.
Just look within.
For your heart is so much bigger than the ways
you seem to
think, hold, share and even maybe a little
embarrassed to care.

Lost souls

When the earth quaked.
When the walls shaked.
Nothing in the air changed.
No one in the room to blame.
Just two lost souls trying to find their ways.

Fishbowl

15

This fish bowl we live in is no way to breathe.
I'm tired of swimming and want to be free.
I want to see what all of this world has to offer
me.

Masks

The game of life, oh what a tricky one.
Scrambling through everything just to find what
you love,
but everyone is wearing masks and won't show
it.

Change

As the autumn leaves wither,
let us rejoice on the mistakes we made.
Remember the faces we shaped.
When the years come to change,
and the memories are washed away,
let us take a moment to relive every forgotten
day.

On the edge.

I've been lost inside my head.
Really i've forgotten what its like to sleep in my
bed.
The girl i used to love just wants me dead,
and all my friends eyes are turning red.
How long am i supposed to go with all these
thoughts scrambled in my brain?
I told them all i just want the love,
fuck the money, fuck the fame.
It's very unfortunate every thinks this is a game.

Love

The harvest moon has passed,
the eclipse shadow has casted upon eden.
We are no longer here nor there my lady,
but everywhere.
You say you want to experience magic, well
just take my hand.

The devil

She has the presence on an angel.
She has the fury of a demon.
She's everything i ever wanted,
She's everything i ever needed.
Trying not to be conceited,
this woman is the one that i am keeping.

so sad

So sad
so sad
never have i been this mad
so sad
so sad
never have i been this glad
oh so, so
sad.

Feelings i've never had.

9 789358 315424